The Bargello Book

The Bargello Book

Frances Salter

A & C Black · London

First published 1993
A & C Black (Publishers) Limited
35 Bedford Row, London WC1R 4JH

ISBN 0-7136-3734-X

© 1993 A & C Black (Publishers) Limited

Typeset by Rowland Phototypesetting Limited,
Bury St Edmunds, Suffolk
Printed in Belgium by
Proost International Book Production

Contents

Acknowledgements

My grateful thanks to Elise Smith without whose help I could never have managed all the descriptions and planning of the designs. Also thanks to Fiona Anderson for her wonderful charts and to Margaret Malcolmson, Margaret Wallis, Margaret Eteen and Pat McLeod for working the sample designs and to Louisa Bellini for typing the manuscript. A special thank you to Sidney Morement for his help too.

Introduction

Bargello, or Florentine needlework, is a quick and easy way of producing attractive contemporary cushion, chair or stool covers. In its simplest form it uses long, straight stitches in various shades of wool on canvas to produce beautiful geometric designs. Simply by counting stitches bargello creates quite astonishing three-dimensional effects without the need for expensive printed patterns. It is easy to master the basic technique as it is quicker than other forms of needlework. It is ideal for anyone who wants to enhance the appearance of a piece of upholstered furniture or make a set of matching cushions, without the necessity of going to classes! Most people find it very therapeutic as it is also easy to pick up and put down at any time, even when travelling.

Bargello is thought to have originated in Europe in the seventeenth century. There are many examples from this period in museums and stately homes in Great Britain, Europe and the United States of America. It was used to make simple purses, samplers, cushions and, of course, to cover upholstered chairs and stools. It was even used for bed hangings. Considering the quality of the materials available it is amazing what early needleworkers achieved.

To suit modern interiors bargello adapts beautifully; either bright clear colours or soft subtle shades merging into one another, or even black, white and grey for the minimal style. It is also ideal for small items such as spectacle cases, scissor cases, luggage straps, doorstops and casual bags. Once you have mastered the basic techniques there are all sorts of possibilities of adapting designs or scaling them up or down to create a very different effect.

Degree of difficulty

Skein symbols have been used to indicate the degree of difficulty of each pattern.

easy

intermediate

difficult

Techniques and Equipment

Unless otherwise specified, start every pattern in the centre of the canvas in order to ensure that the finished design is symmetrical. Do not use excessively long lengths of yarn, repeated passing through the canvas will weaken the yarn. If it does seem to be thin it is better to discard it. Approximately 30 in (75 cm) is a suitable length. When you start a length of yarn pull it through from the back until only about 1½ in (4 cm) remains at the back of the canvas. Holding this with your other hand at the back of the work, catch it into subsequent stitches as you work along the row, thus securing it firmly and neatly. Do not let yarn run behind finished work of a lighter shade. To finish a strand of yarn, pull the last couple of inches to the back of the canvas, and thread it back and forth through the work (of the same colour) that you have just completed. Cut off any excess close to the canvas.

There is no need to work bargello on a frame and of course it is far easier to carry the work around without one.

Stitching method

Bargello creates a pattern by varying the grouping and size of the stitches. All stitches are vertical. Begin by bringing the yarn to the front of the canvas at the bottom of the stitch. Count the number of threads (horizontal threads in the canvas) and insert the needle at the top of the stitch. Because the next stitch to be made begins at the bottom again you will always be leaving substantial yarn at the back of the canvas. Not only does this make the front of the canvas look better, but it also strengthens the finished work and ensures that it will wear well. Try not to pull the yarn too tightly, keep an even, light tension which will lessen the chance of the canvas showing through.

Canvas

When you are embarking on a project that will require hours of work and last for years, do not try and save money on the materials. Good materials look better, last longer and are a pleasure to work with.

Always use good quality single-thread (mono) canvas. You will obtain the best results if the canvas is made of polished cotton threads that feel smooth to the touch. Interlock canvas, in which the threads are split and twisted round each other where they intersect, is less satisfactory, and double thread canvas is not suitable because the double threads hold the stitches apart.

You should start with a piece of canvas that will leave at least 2 in (5 cm) of unworked canvas on all sides of the finished needlework. You will need to leave a larger margin for a chairseat or stool cover. After the canvas has been cut to the correct size, finish off the edges to prevent them from fraying and catching on the yarn as you stitch. Either hem the canvas on your sewing machine (don't forget to allow for this when estimating the size of the canvas) or tack by hand. Masking tape tends to come off after a while.

Mark the centre of the canvas lightly with a pencil and draw lines equidistant from the centre in between the threads of canvas. When marking out a chairseat or stool cover take careful measurements. For a drop-in seat, measure from front to back, across the back and across the front just into the wood. For an overstuffed seat, measure the top and add the drops leaving out the corners.

Choosing the gauge of canvas

The gauge (number of threads to the inch) of the canvas will determine the scale of the design and the durability of the needlework. The smaller the gauge, the finer the pattern and the better the wearing characteristics of the work. A chairseat would be best done on 18 mesh canvas, although 14 mesh might be alright if the chair has very little use. A cushion cover, however, could be done on anything from 10 to 18 mesh, and you could exploit this flexibility by doing the same pattern on different meshes to make cushions of different sizes and effects that look marvellous together.

Most canvas sizes are generally available in 40 in (1 m) widths (some in 27 in (70 cm) widths) in white or beige (antique); there is no difference in the quality, but beige may be preferable if you are using predominantly dark colours.

Yarns

Choosing the right yarn for the canvas is quite important. You should use 100% wool. Do not use synthetic or knitting yarns as they are not designed for canvaswork. The yarn you use should generously cover the canvas, there is nothing worse than bits of canvas showing through the finished stitching.

Canvas gauge	Yarns to use
18	Stranded cotton or cotton perle
16, 18	1 strand tapestry wool/3 strands crewel
15, 16	2 strands Persian/DMC
13, 14	4 strands crewel
12, 13	All 3 strands of Persian
10	5 strands crewel/3 + 1 strands Persian/ 2 strands tapestry wool.

Yarns generally available

4-ply tapestry wool
Single indivisible strand. *Appleton* have over 400 shades available in small skeins or more economical 25 g hanks (just under 1 oz). *Coats* have a wide range available in small skeins. Limited range available in larger 20 g hanks. *DMC* have a slightly thicker 4-ply tapestry wool. Wide range available in small skeins. Limited range available in larger hanks.

Crewel
Fine 2-ply wool useful for any size canvas, use as many strands as you need to cover the canvas. *Appleton* have the same range as for their 4-ply tapestry wool.

Persian yarn
The wool has three strands which are easily separated. *Paterna* have over 400 shades available in small skeins or 4 oz (115 g) hanks. Generally sold in cut lengths.

Stranded cotton/Cotton perle
Ideal for small items or highlighting. *Coats* and *DMC* have a wide range available in small skeins.

Quantities of yarn needed

As a rough guide, most of the 8 in square samples shown in this book use very little yarn. A half hank of Appleton tapestry wool (or 3 small skeins) of each shade is ample. Slightly more if only 3 shades used.

A 16 in cushion would use approximately 4–5 25 g (4 oz in all) hanks of wool or 25 or more small skeins. It is best to buy sufficient yarn for your project as dye lots do vary.

Needles

Tapestry needles have a blunt point. The larger the canvas the larger the needle. For an 18 mesh canvas you should use a size 22 or a 20 needle. The eye should be large enough to accommodate the yarn without fraying it and small enough to slip through the holes of the canvas without unduly distorting it. For thicker wool and coarser canvas use size 18 needles.

Blocking

If you have worked fairly evenly there should be very little distortion of the canvas. But it may still need to be blocked square. A good press with a damp cloth may be sufficient. Or you need a clean flat board covered with clean lining paper, or blotting paper, drawing pins and a steam iron. Pin the canvas, right side down, from the centre top outwards, lining it up with the edge of the board. Repeat on the opposite edge and sides. Steam iron with a damp cloth and leave to dry thoroughly before removing from the board.

Finishing

Unless you are experienced at piping you may prefer to have your cushion made up professionally. If tackling it yourself, I suggest a non-shiny fabric and a matching cord may be the easiest way to finish your cushion.

Items for upholstery should be blocked by an experienced upholsterer before being applied to the chair or stool.

Note on charts

Each background line of the chart represents one thread of canvas. The symbols on each chart represent the different shades used. No specific colours are indicated as it is up to the needleworker to choose their own colours. If the colours used are required, they are all available in Appleton tapestry and crewel wool. All the designs were worked on 18 mesh single canvas, if a coarser mesh were used the motifs would be increased in size.

Baubles

Number of colours: four shades of one colour (baubles) and three shades of another (diamonds). **Thread count:** all stitches are over four threads in steps of two and groups of one to four stitches.

If you turn the pattern upside down, you get a completely different effect – one of the nice things about bargello.

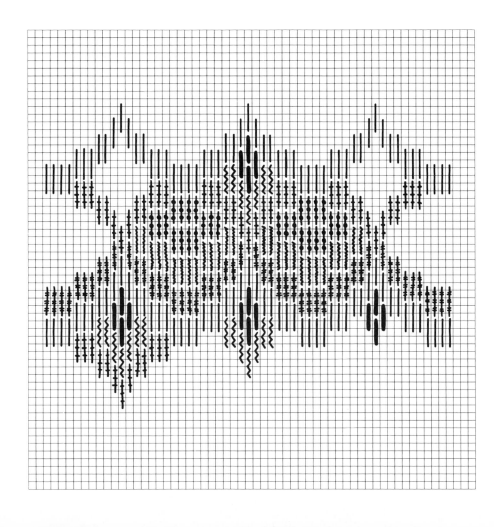

Chainmail

Number of colours: three. **Thread count:** all stitches are over four threads, either in blocks of five or as single stitches in steps of two.

It is a good idea to thread a needle with each of the outline colours and keep both the colours going at once so that you avoid mistakes where the colours cross. You can then go back and fill in with the third colour.

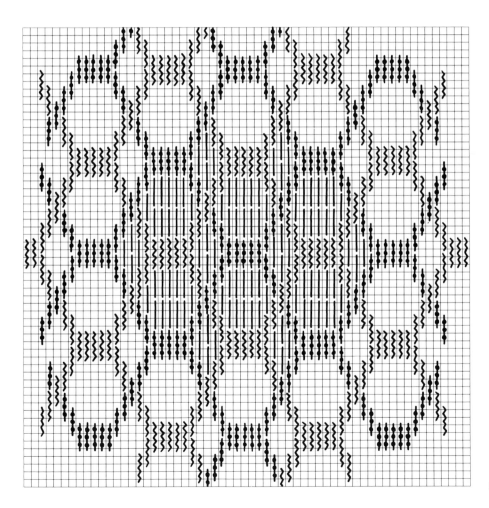

Chevrons

Number of colours: four shades of one colour. **Thread count:** over six threads in steps of five or steps of one.

Start in the centre and work first to one side and then to the other to form an entire row. It is best to start with the darkest colour. Then continue with each new shade from one end of the row to the other.

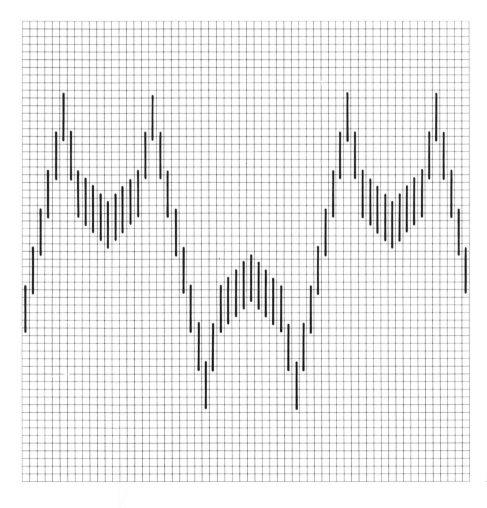

Circles and Diamonds

Number of colours: the sample is worked in three colours, but you could use four. **Thread count:** over four threads in steps of two, from single stitches to blocks of four.

Work the circles first, from the outline in, and the diamonds will form themselves.

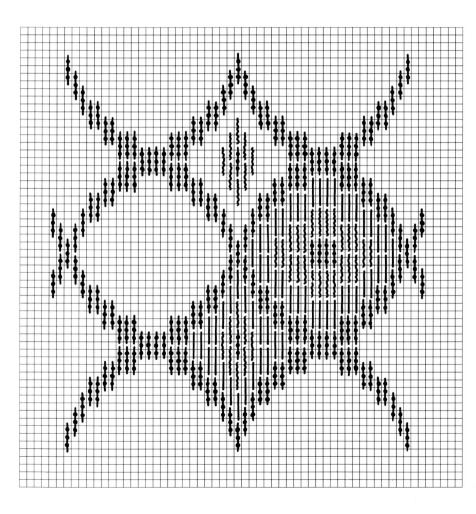

Cubes

Number of colours: six shades of one colour, or five shades of one colour plus a darker colour for centre. **Thread count:** pairs of stitches, all over four threads, in steps of two.

This simple, wonderfully three-dimensional pattern is equally suitable in modern or traditional decorative schemes. Start with the palest colour, outline a couple of boxes completely and then fill in with the other shades. Carry on in the same way, outlining and filling. Avoid doing a lot of the palest shade before filling in, because you may find that you have made a mistake somewhere along the way, and the pattern is no longer repeating itself correctly.

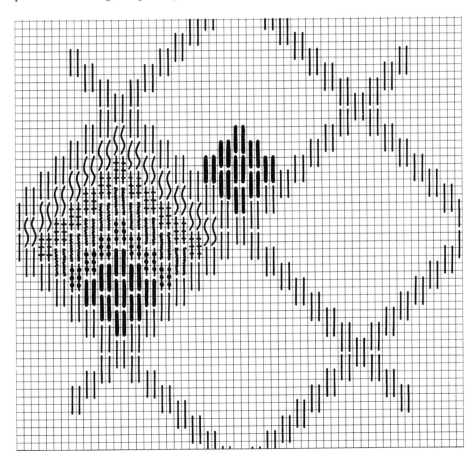

15

Diamond Lights

Number of colours: four shades of one colour. **Thread count:** single stitches over four threads in steps of two.

Start working the outline from the centre then fill in with the other shades. You could easily reverse the infill to create a different effect.

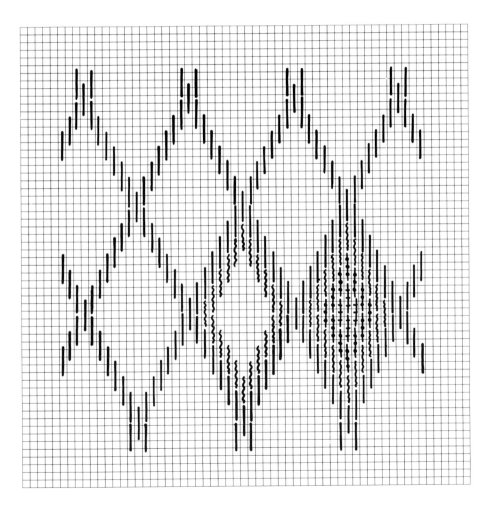

Diamond Panes

Number of colours: three. **Thread count:** the outline is over four threads. The next row is over two, three and four threads and the centre of the diamond is over two, four and six threads. All stitches in steps of one.

Work some of the zig zag outline and then fill in with the diamonds.

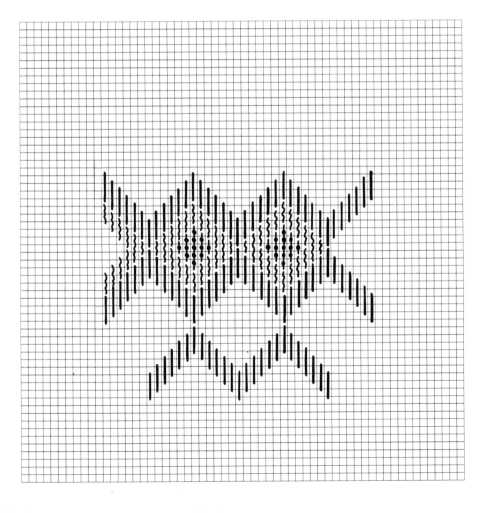

Elliptical Diamonds

Number of colours: five shades of one colour. **Thread count:** over four threads in steps of two. In single stitches and blocks of two, three and four stitches, starting in the centre, work an area of outline colour and then fill in with the other shades.

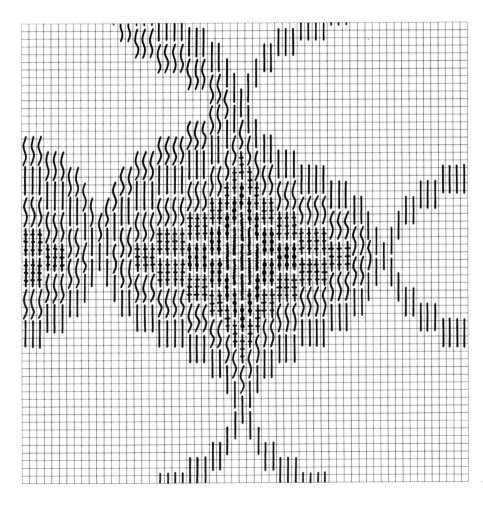

Hearts

Number of colours: five shades of one colour and two shades of a contrasting colour. **Thread count:** over four threads in steps of two, from single stitches to groups of four.

Work the palest colour first, outlining the combined heart and diamond shapes. Then fill in the heart colours, then the diamonds. For a different effect, you could reverse the shading on the hearts, using the darkest shade for the outline.

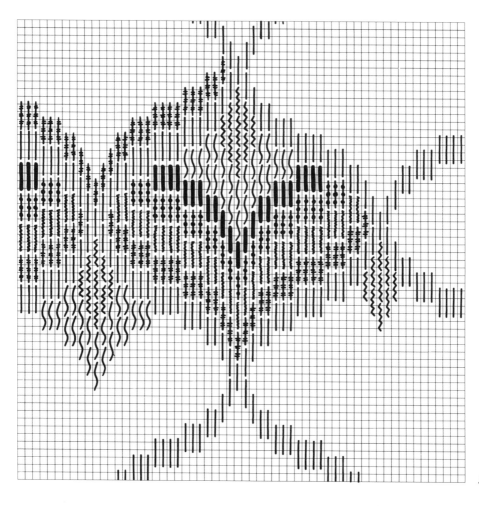

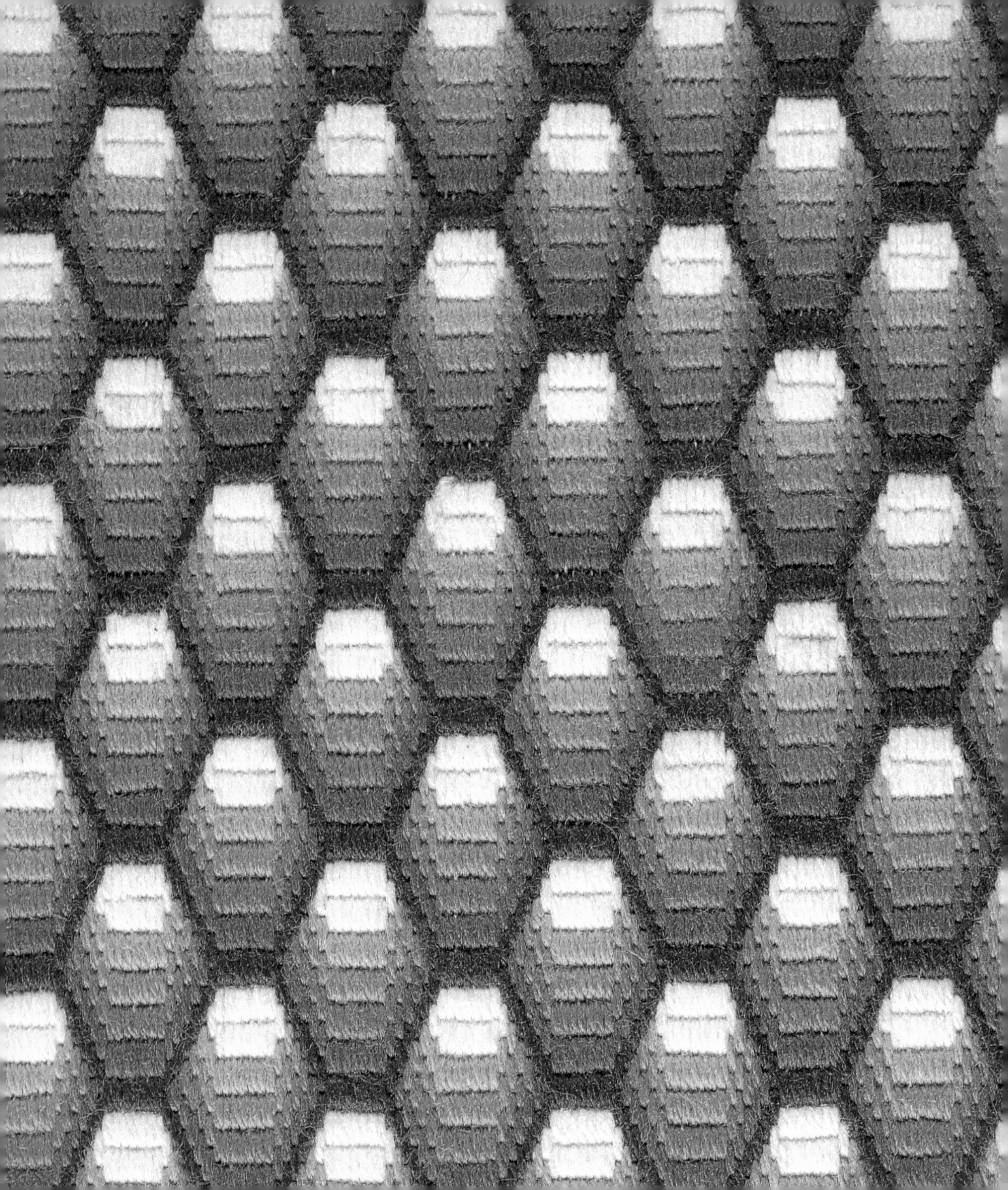

Honeycomb

Number of colours: six shades of one colour, ranging from dark to very pale. **Thread count:** over four threads in steps of two, in singles or groups of seven.

Do a central portion of the outline and fill in. This is safer than trying to complete the whole of the outlining at once.

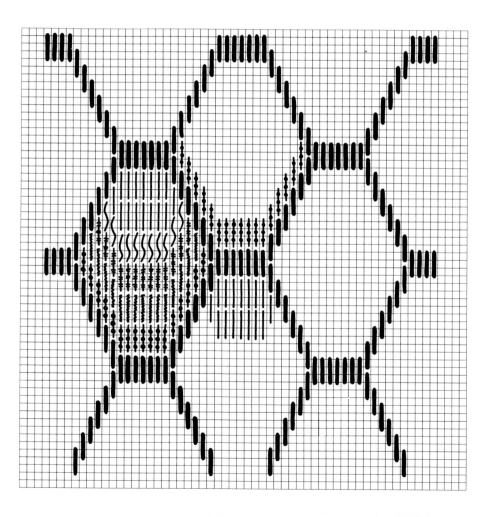

Jacobean Spires

Number of colours: one base colour. Two shades of one colour and five shades of another colour. **Thread count:** single stitches over six threads and single stitches over two threads in steps of one.

Start with an outline row and count very carefully. Usually two long stitches are followed by two short stitches but, when you reach the peaks, you may have to stitch three short stitches or three long stitches. If in doubt follow the threads of colour vertically below the stitch you are going to make. You will see that the repeat is two short stitches always followed by two long stitches.

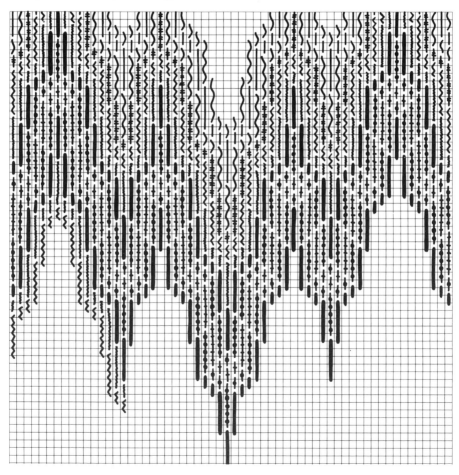

Leaves

Number of colours: three shades of one colour and a contrasting colour for the stem. **Thread count:** outline is over four threads in steps of one. The leaf shape is over two in steps of one, except for the 'stem' which is a single stitch over four threads.

Work some rows of outline, being careful to leave a gap for the stem, and then fill them in.

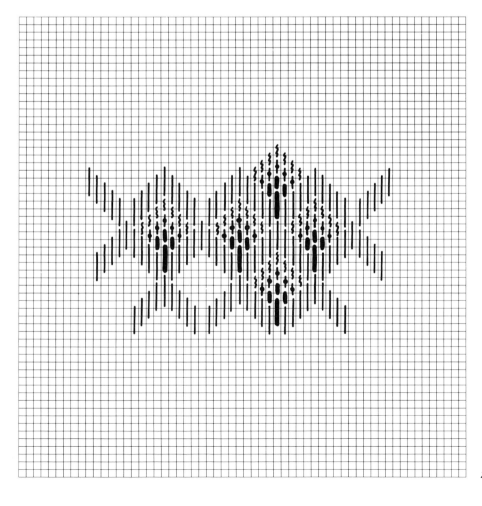

Lightning

Number of colours: five shades of one colour plus three of another.
Thread count: single stitches over four threads in steps of two.

Start in the centre and work the outline. Then fill in with each shade.
This design can be varied greatly by using more shades and varying the
proportions used.

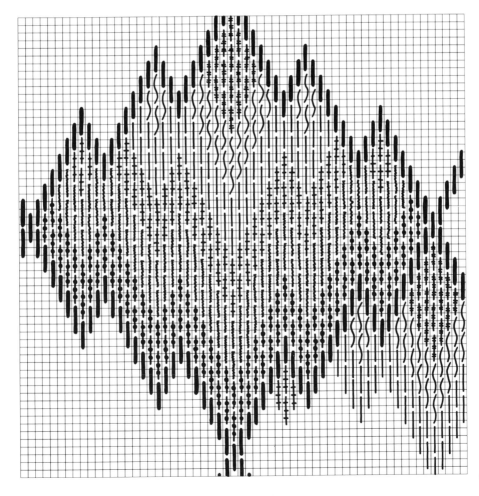

Little Basketweave

Number of colours: three. **Thread count:** pairs of stitches over four threads in steps of two.

The pattern will take form more easily if you thread a needle with every colour (three needles) and do each shade as you come to it, rather than trying to complete a whole strip of one colour by leaving gaps where the different colours intersect.

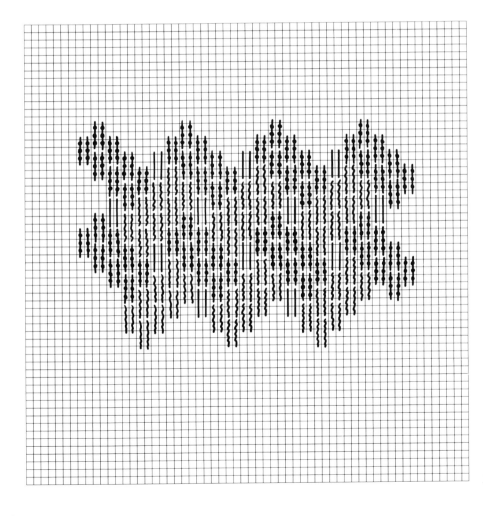

Little Boxes

Number of colours: three. **Thread count:** groups of two stitches over four threads in steps of two.

Establish the outline with the darkest colour and fill in with the other two shades.

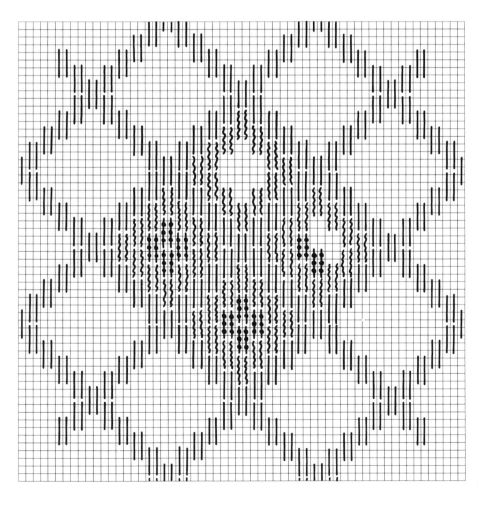

Mini Check

Number of colours: three. **Thread count:** pairs of stitches over four in steps of two.

Start in the centre with the outline colour and work a portion of the outline before filling in the diamond shapes.

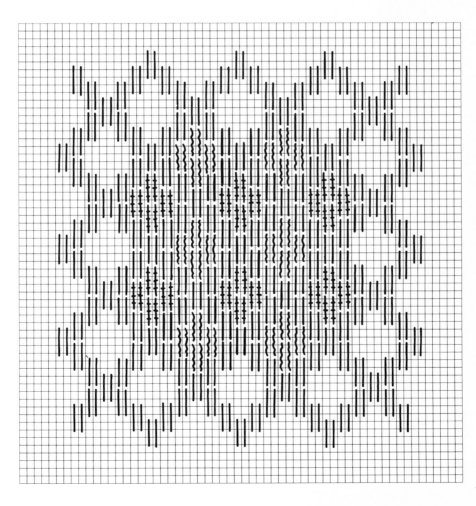

Northern Lights

Number of colours: the sample is worked in four shades of two colours. You can use as many different colours and shades as you like depending on the size of the finished canvas. **Thread count:** single stitches over four threads in steps of two.

This is a very easy pattern once the first row has been carefully done. The effect can differ greatly according to the distribution of colour. Start the first row in the centre of the canvas and work first to one side and then to the other to form a complete row. Continue with the other shades from one side of the canvas to the other.

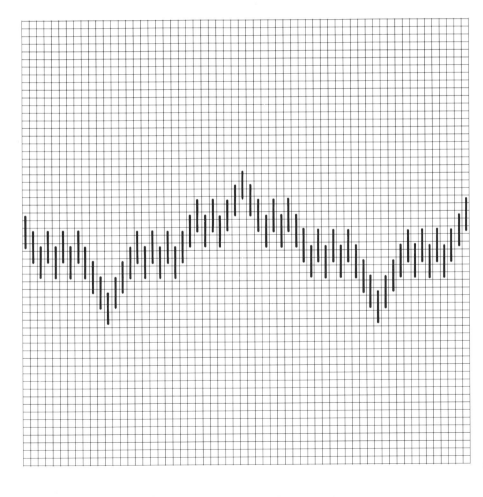

Open Basketweave

Number of threads: four shades each of two colours and one additional contrasting colour (total of nine). **Thread count:** pairs of stitches over four threads in steps of two.

The pattern will take form more easily if you thread a needle with every colour (nine needles) doing each shade as you come to it, rather than trying to do a whole strip of one colour and leaving gaps where the other colours intersect. You will inevitably leave the wrong size gap somewhere along the way! Using the darkest colour for the spots will create a more pronounced three-dimensional effect than using the lightest colour.

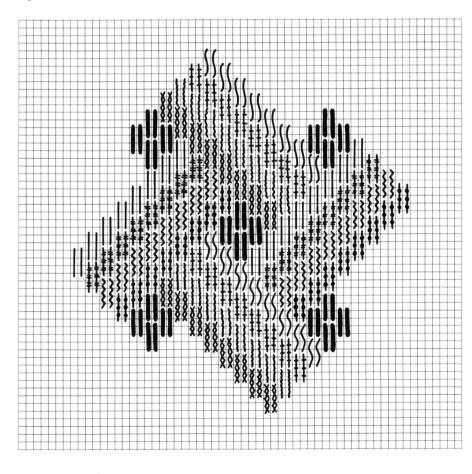

Peacock Feathers

Number of colours: four shades of one colour (circles) and three shades of another (diamonds). **Thread count:** the stitches are always over four threads in steps of two, but are in groups of one, two or three stitches.

Work the outline of the circles first and then fill in the other colours.

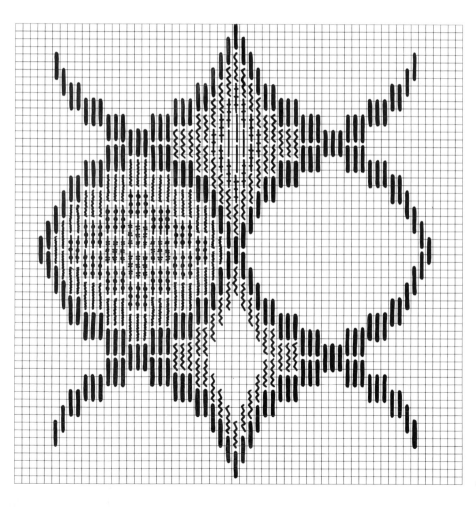

Petals

Number of colours: five shades of one colour. **Thread count:** over four threads in steps of two, in blocks of one to four.

Starting in the middle of the canvas, establish the outline with the darkest colour and then fill in with the other shades. A dramatically different effect would be achieved by reversing the order of the shades and using the lightest shade for the outline and the darkest shade for the middle.

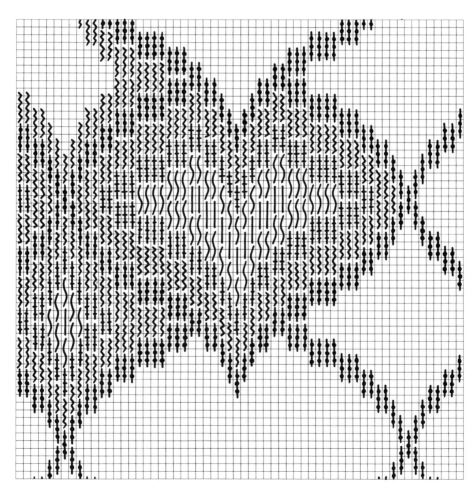

Pointed Curves

Number of colours: the sample uses five shades of one colour, but this can be varied. **Thread count:** over six threads in steps of three, from single stitches to blocks of four.

Start in the centre of the canvas and work first to one side and then to the other for the first row. Continue with each new shade from one end of the row to the other.

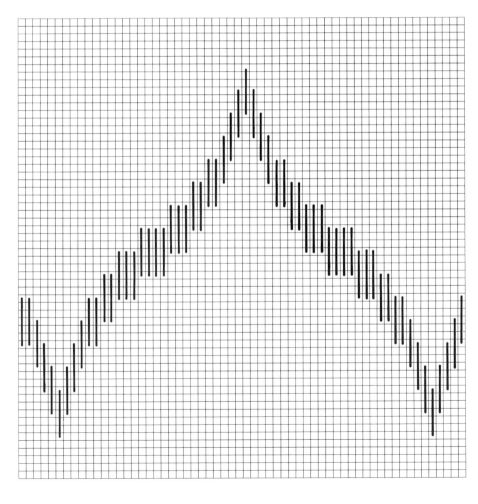

Points and Arches

Number of colours: four shades of one colour (or more). **Thread count:** over four threads in steps of two, in groups from one to five stitches.

Start in the middle of the canvas and work first to one side and then to the other to form a complete row. Continue with the other shades from one side of the canvas to the other.

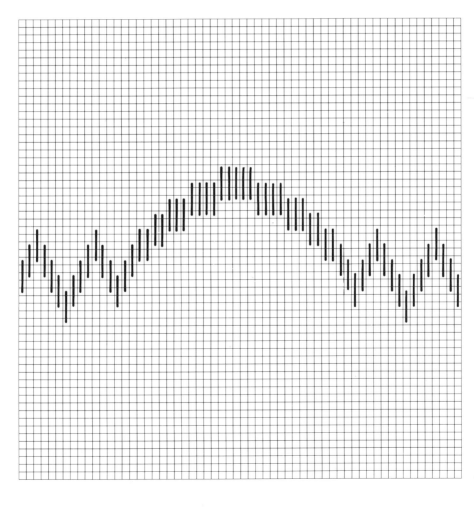

Psychedelic Zig Zags

Number of colours: five shades of one colour. **Thread count:** over four threads in steps of one thread.

Start in the centre of the canvas and work first to one side and then to the other for the first row. Continue with each new shade from one end of the row to the other.

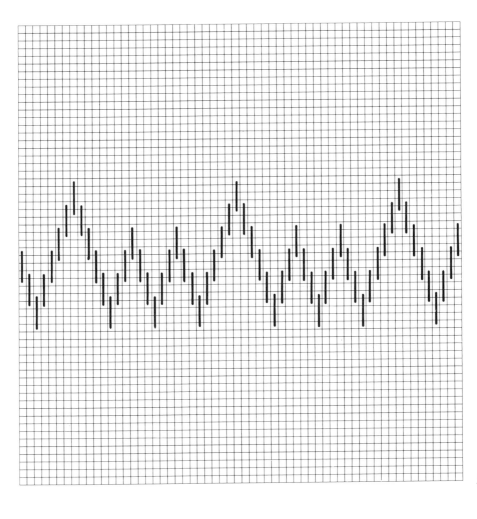

Quills

Number of colours: five shades of one colour. **Thread count:** single stitches over four threads. In steps of two with a block of five stitches over four threads.

Set up the outline and fill in with the other shades. Watch for the single stitch at the top of the point.

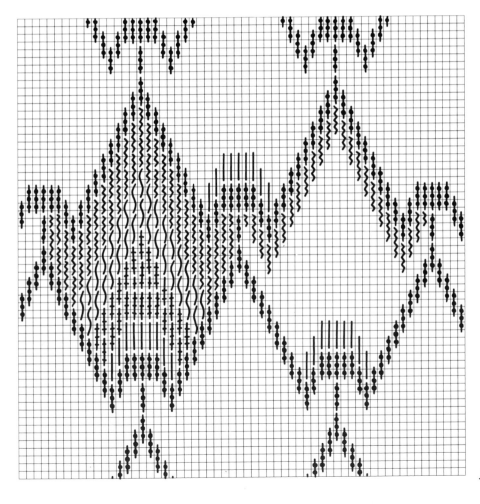

Quilted Diamonds

Number of colours: four shades of one colour. **Thread count:** the outline consists of single stitches over four threads in steps of one. The inner single stitches over one, two, three or four threads in steps of one. Central single stitches over two, four, six, eight and ten threads.

Work some of the main outline starting in the centre then fill with the other shades.

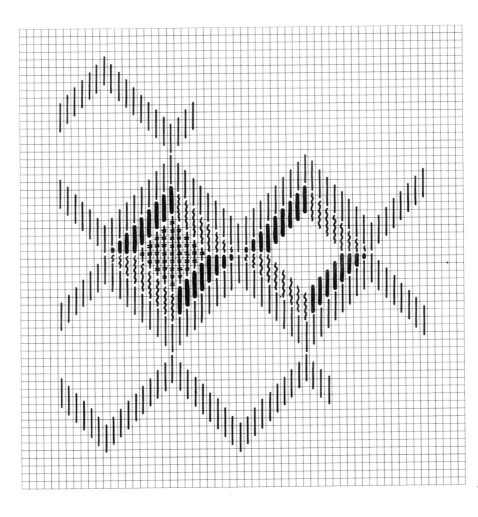

Ripples ———————————————————

Number of colours: six (any number will do). **Thread count:** over four threads in steps of two, in blocks of one to four.

The first row should be worked from top right to bottom left (if you are right–handed) and all the other rows simply follow on.

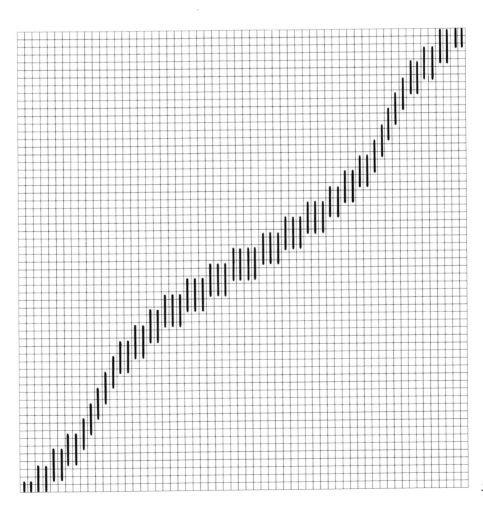

Shells

Number of colours: seven shades of one colour. **Thread count:** mainly over four threads, but watch for the occasional stitches over six or over two threads.

Starting in the middle of the canvas, as usual, work a portion of the outline (in the darkest shade) then fill in the other shades.

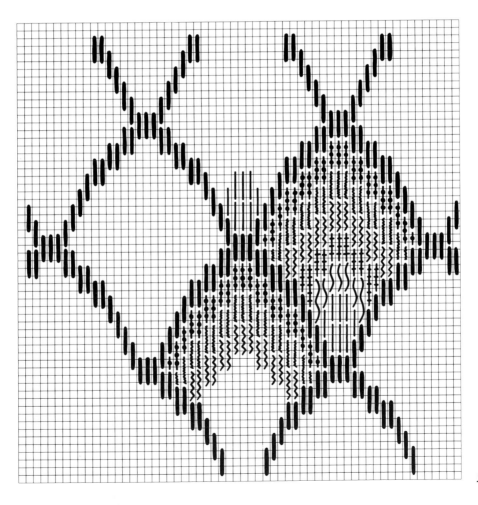

Stepping Stones

Number of colours: four shades of one colour. **Thread count:** over four threads in steps of two, in single stitches, pairs and blocks of nine stitches.

This pattern is dramatically different depending on which way you look at it. But it is worked with the canvas held so that the effect is of vertical stripes. Working in the darkest colour do the outline first and then fill in.

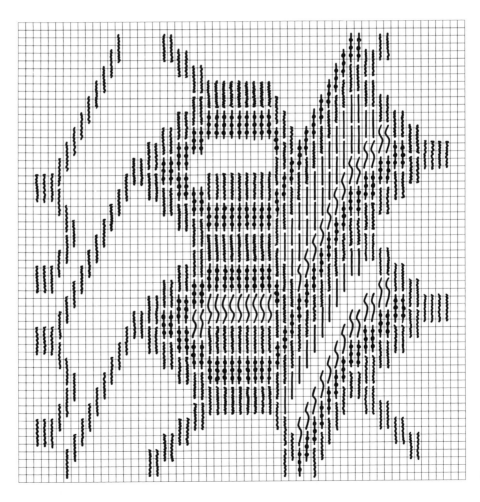

Three-dimensional Boxes

Number of colours: three shades of three or four different colours.
Thread count: single stitches worked over four threads in steps of
two, with filling in stitches over two threads. Top and side panels are
worked over four threads in steps of one.

Starting in the centre follow the chart carefully, completing one colour
box before starting another. Note: four stitches use the same hole. This
is a useful design for using up odd scraps of wool to create a three-
dimentional effect.

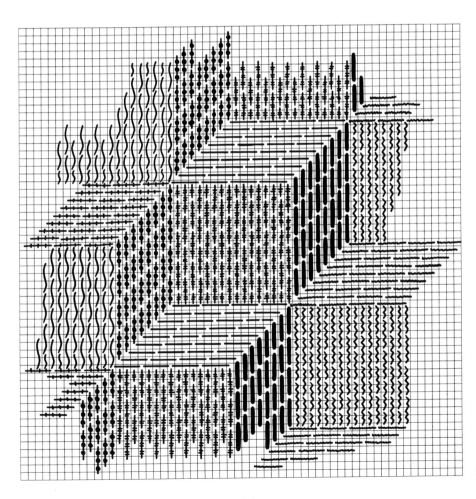